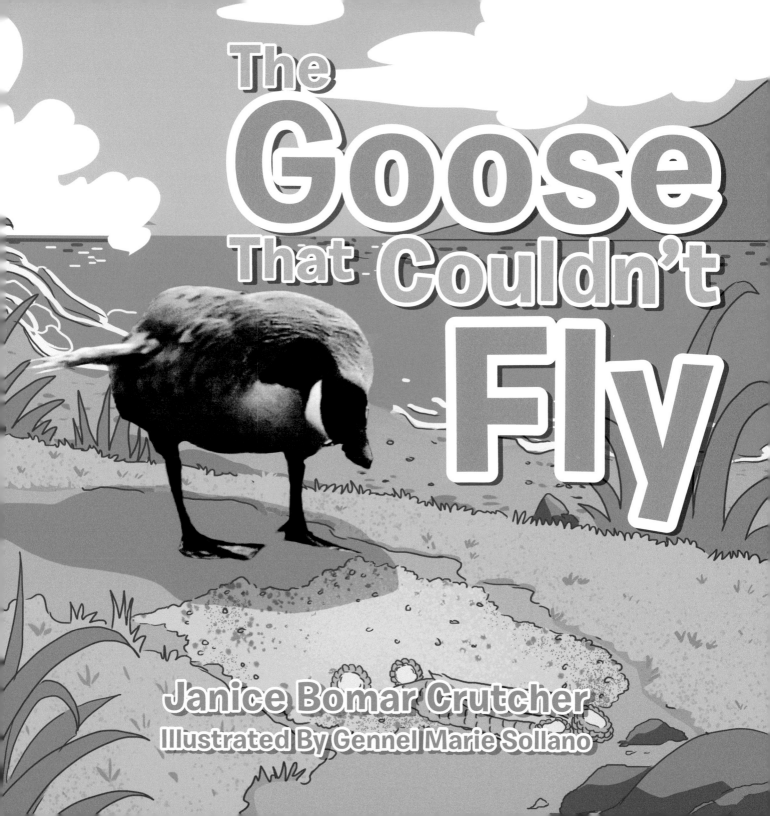

The Goose That Couldn't Fly

Janice Bomar Crutcher

Illustrated By Gennel Marie Sollano

To order additional copies of this book, contact:
Xlibris
844-714-8691
www.Xlibris.com
Orders@Xlibris.com

ISBN: Softcover   978-1-6698-7818-6
         EBook   978-1-6698-7817-9

Print information available on the last page

Rev. date: 05/17/2023

The Goose That Couldn't Fly

This is "Mac" The Canada Goose

This is "Gracie" The Muscovy Duck

Let me introduce myself. My name is Mac. I am a Canada goose. I have a black head and neck with a white chinstrap. The rest of my feathers are known as plumage. They are brownish, gray and black in color.

My journey started in Canada. This was where I was born. We stayed in Canada until the winter got so cold. Just imagine snow all around us. We headed South so the weather would not be as cold. This is called migration. All my friends and parents started our journey from Canada to Tennessee. This was the distance of 800 miles.

When traveling we fly in a "V" pattern. If you hear the geese look up to the sky. You will see our "V" pattern. The more experienced geese lead the flock.

On our journey we would sleep in the water. My friends would stand watch so we could sleep. We exchanged watches so the others could sleep. Each shift was the guards to protect us from predators. Predators are animals that hunt for a meat source for their diet. Examples of predators are tigers, bears, sharks, weasels, wolves, mountain lions, hawks and coyotes.

Each shift had to be very watchful for the predators. If a predator got into the water while we were sleeping it would ripple the water to awaken us to danger. Most of the time the guards would awaken us.

Our migration period begins in September or October. That is when we relocate to North America heading south. We as a group would fly by day or night depending on the weather and the brightness of the moon. Migrating geese can fly 1,500 miles (about 2414.02 km) in a 24-hour period. A mile is measured as 5,280 feet (about 1.61 km). Think of an example of 24 hours. This would be 6:00 a.m. to 6:00 a.m. the next day. With speeds of 40 miles in an hour or 60 minutes. Remember for us to get to Tennessee we had to travel over 800 miles. If we got caught in a tailwind, we could fly around 70 miles per hour. A tailwind is the air current of the wind blowing in the direction we are flying.

Big groups like the one I was flying in are called a gaggle of geese. When we landed onto the field, we would get loud and noisy.

On our journey we were flying over Kentucky Lake. We flew into a bay. This is a picturesque and charming bay community on the lake water's edge. On my flight into Kentucky Lake Bay, I must have hit something in the water. All I know because of this I couldn't fly anymore. I played and swam in the water around the shoreline. Sometimes I would just sit on the bank to rest.

At this point I was thought of as different by the other geese like me. I couldn't fly so I stayed in the bay. The other geese were not nice to me. They would not allow me to be in their group because I was different. They would fly away and leave me all alone. I was so lonely being by myself for many days.

Then one day this ugly duck appeared. To me she was beautiful. She was considered different like me by the other geese because she didn't look like them. She had brown, white and black feathers. She didn't look like me, She was a Muscovy duck. Just like me they wanted nothing to do with her.

Please let me introduce her. Her name is Gracie. She became my buddy. We would swim everywhere in the bay. Just because you are different do not let others bully you by being mean or make you sad. She became my best friend. We did everything together. She cannot fly very high at all. We swam a lot.

Gracie would always keep the other geese from eating my food on the beach. She would chase them into the water to keep them away from my corn to make sure I got to eat each day.

Keep in mind I had no way to fly to a corn field for food to eat. Then one day this nice lady began to feed us. She would put out fresh crushed corn by the water for us to feed on every day.

This was a delight to Gracie and me. It would be like someone carrying you to get a big ice cream cone. What a joy for you as the corn was for Gracie and me. Around the bay were Condos. A condo is a building or complex owned by different people. They have their own private beach. Everyone is so nice to feed us. I am sure enjoying my new home with my new friend Gracie.

Some days I would swim around looking for new adventures. Exploring places around the bay for Gracie and me to do. After a couple of days, we would meet back up and go exploring the places I had found around the shoreline.

Just because you are different doesn't let anyone get you feeling down about yourself. As you can see Gracie and I are so different to the other geese we found each other. We didn't let the other geese bully us. As our journey continues, I will let you know of all our adventures.

Thank you for reading my story. Don't let anyone bully you just because you are different. You are special and important. Never forget this.... YOU MATTER!

Thank you for reading my story. Don't let anyone bully you just because you are different. You are special and important. Never forget this.... YOU MATTER!

Printed in the United States
by Baker & Taylor Publisher Services